Ecstasy of Life

## Also by Donald W. Grant

Poetry

*Shades of Life*
*Echoes of Life*
*Silence of Life*
*Reflections of Life*
*Trials of Life*

Non-Fiction

*M.A.G.A.: Making America Go Awry*

# Ecstasy of Life

*A Collection of Poems*

*By*
*Donald W. Grant*

**DC**
D2C Perspectives

ISBN: 978-1-943142-61-3

# Table of Contents

*To Billy Collins, il miglio fabbor, who reminds me through his poetry that it is the simple things that make up the ecstasy of life*

# Something Good To Say

Sitting at my desk on a dreary, rainy day,
It would be easy to be depressed,
To find nothing good to say.

It is cold outside, the sky
Overcast, covered in a light gray.
The sun refusing to appear.

Can I find something good to say?

Seems like this is a metaphor
For just about any day.
It is easy to focus on the bad,

Hard to find good things to say.
Seems only when times are bad
We get on our knees to pray.

Ever think just maybe, God
Would like to hear something good today!

With that in mind, these poems

Will look at life in a different way.

Observing the ecstasy of life,
Finding something good to say.

# Ode To The Heron

If you were not paying attention
You would go right by her
Motionless in a field of brown grass
She resembles a tall reed.

In all the mornings I have passed
By this field on my way to the ocean
These past few are the first time
She has appeared.

Where she came from, I do not know
Is she nesting or just pausing
from her journey to somewhere afar?
If I could get close enough to hear
And if she had the ability to speak
There are so many questions I would ask

What brings you here to this field?
Where have you been and where are you going?
Have you read any good books lately?
Who is your favorite poet?

She is a marvel of nature with
That long neck and skinny legs
Standing on the earth looking so fragile
Yet once taking flight, as graceful
As the prima ballerina in Swan Lake.

# Shark

A surfer was killed by a shark today
Why it attacked no one can say

Maybe is was the slick wet suit
That resembled the skin of a seal

Or maybe the surfer kicked and
paddled with too much zeal

Signs went up, the beach was closed
Five days access will be blocked
As if in five days the shark will go away

What makes them think he won't want to stay

Around just to see if more food appears?
Maybe to him a surfer is a delicacy

So, in five days when the surfers
And swimmers go back out
We will just have to wait and see

It is funny to me how surprised people can be
At the news of a shark swimming in our bay

Do people forget where sharks make their home?
The ocean is the natural place for sharks to stay

So maybe the surfers who ride on the foam
Need to remember they are the ones invading

To the shark the sea is simply his home.

# Simple Pleasures

Having tread upon this earth
For just over seventy-two years
I have come to appreciate the small
Things in life as opposed to the grandiose

Holding a book in my hand
Be it a thriller, political, or poetry
Feeling the texture of paper as my
Eyes delight in each phrase
A feeling a Kindle can never duplicate

Walking along the shore as the tide
Washes over my feet, my wife
By my side matching stride for stride
Mostly silent, deep in thought with
The occasional comment on the oddity of life

Together on the couch as evening arrives
Enjoying the release a TV show brings
From the reality of daily life
A bowl of popcorn between us and
Perhaps a glass of wine or shot of Scotch

To sit on the roof deck out of the sun
Under an umbrella to shade my fragile skin
Yet still feeling the warmth of the day
A cigar in one hand, wine in the other

The music of the 60's the only sound

These are the things that bring me pleasure
Simple moments like these forever to treasure

# The Colored Houses

They have stood facing east across Monterey Bay
For over ninety-six years, still being used today
As condos to hold tourists who have come to stay
To relax, eat amazing seafood, and to just play

In the sand, in the water, or just to lay
Out in the sun, spending the day away
From the stress they feel most every day

They were originally built to mimic the atmosphere
And sense of Venice, a bit of Europe here.
Painted bright pastel colors, these condos appear
To have been painted by a hippie from another year.

Staring across the sand they have seen their share
Of surfers challenging waves, agile and with no fear
Multitudes of beach goers coming year after year
To frolic in the water, to lay out, or to just drink
beer

Occasionally, they have seen whales breaching in
pairs
As the tourists gasp in awe or tremble in fear
As a great white will sometimes appear

They have watched over the years as across the bay
The Cement Ship has been in a state of disarray

The wind and rain and tide have caused the ship to decay
And what was once the pride of Seacliff is slowly fading away

But today the colored houses of Capitola still stand
And every summer are still in great demand
As long as the tide remains and there is just
a little bit of sand
They will attract beachgoers, some beet red,
some tanned.

# The Lamp

My father gave me a lamp when I was nine
Made of brass with two fluorescent tubes
That even today, work just fine

The old-fashioned kind that needs the switch
Held for a time so the gas can ignite
And compared to lamps of today may
Not be quite as bright

But it has survived multitudes of moves
And multitudes of wives and lit my way
Through whatever life threw my way

Helping me early on with simple math
And book reports of a variety of reads
To quadratic equations, calculus, and
Finally, helping me get my doctor's degree

The lamp is heavy, weighing at least eight pounds
My father took it from his office
when no one was around.
Now sixty-four years have passed and my lamp
Is still working, and on my desk can always be
found.

# Cheese

There is a quote that is going around
By G.K. Chesterton, a man of renown.

He said, "Poets have been mysteriously
Silent on the subject of cheese."
With respect to G.K., and your permission,
Let me correct that, if you please.

Poets may not like the word cheese,
After all with what does it rhyme,
Maybe trees, bees, or knees.

Would a poet write, 'I crossed the seven seas
Searching the world for the best cheese?"
Or, "On the top of my stew of potatoes
and peas,
I sprinkled loads of Parmesan cheese."

A poet must think hard if they're going
to pay homage,
To all the great cheeses, which does not
include cottage.

So to G.K. Chesterton I simply want to say,
"This poet has now opined on cheese, so
I guess, I'll be on my way."

# Reminiscing

Regardless of the season
The bridge is covered in snow,
The river partly with ice.

The air so cold your breath freezes,
No outer garment enough to keep out the
chill from penetrating to your bones.

As the days go by, no one crosses
The bridge making footprints in the snow,
No skater is ever on the ice nor
Boat ever on the river where it still flows.

Every day I sit and gaze at the bridge
Covered in snow, the river partly with ice.

And from my room in California I recall
The time I was in Des Moines taking the
Picture, now framed and hung on my wall.

# Even-Stevens

Standing in the park watching
My granddaughter playing in the sand
A bucket beside her, a shovel in her hand

Methodically, she scoops the sand
Filling the bucket, one shovel at a time
Then dumping it, then filling it time after time

She is content, her life is just fine
My thoughts interrupted by a bell across the way
I look up to see children being released
to go out and play

They pour out of their classroom, a break in their
day like hornets escaping a nest, chaotic
A teacher rounds them up, they now look robotic

The play is structured, they're not free to frolic
My mind flashes back to my own school days
When we were left alone to decide what to play

We played our own games, more fun in a way
Flipping baseball cards, calling odds or evens
Sometimes winning, sometimes losing,
sometimes even-stevens

This was not gambling, I might want to mention

I was pretty good and amassed quite a collection
Which had I kept to this day would be worth a
fortune

So enough talk of the past, that was not my
Intention. Standing in the park watching
My granddaughter playing the old days were
Better, that is all I am saying.

# Beach Walk

Like an alarm set to awaken
We start out on our beach walk
Every morning like clockwork

A four-mile round trip that
Begins our day, setting the mood
For whatever the day may bring

A refreshing trek across the sand
Observing the occasional whale or
School of dolphins, for sure a
Seal or two, stalking us from the
Rolling waves as we walk

The fresh air and sea breeze
Invigorating, unless the wind
Brings in the stench of the Concrete Ship
Covered in the digested remnants left by
Pelicans, seagulls, and a multitude of sea fowl

As exhilarating as the beach walk can be
Maybe, it is sometimes the two blocks
We cross before the beach that evokes emotion

Like the two bags of dog-poo that
Lies in the gutter, that no one wants to remove
Like the pile of dog-poo in the middle of the street

That appears without fail, fresh and pungent

Like the worker bees that speed down the street
Heading to their hives, ignoring the lines and signs
Of the crosswalk where we have the right of way

Like the monstrous garbage truck
That we have to dodge as it veers
Across the road to pick up a dumpster

Every morning before we reach
The serenity and Zen of the beach
We are reminded daily of just how much
The actions of humanity reeks.

# Birthday

How old are you?
A question that is not easy to answer
Not that I don't know
Just that sometimes I have to stop and think

As of this writing I am seventy-two
About to be seventy-three and
There-in lies the problem

I started to say I was seventy-three
Because I will be when actually I am not
So when asked, I have to think of now not then

How old are you?
Brings up thoughts of when
I was born, and never when I was created
Let's just say my parents had a great Thanksgiving

How old are you?
Also makes me think of what else
Was happening the year I was born
It was a busy time

The first UFO's were spotted
The Air Force was born and
The CIA became our nation's spies

Man broke the speed of sound
And the transistor was invented
Jackie Robinson broke the racial barrier
And Henry Ford is no longer around

Drive-in movies were the rage
Could that be where I was created?
Or was I dropped off by the UFO
Either way, '47 was my debut on the world stage.

# My Poet's Window

Okay Mr. Collins, I took your advice.
I went to the window in the front
of the house
And looking out decided to write this poem.

There are things that I see that are
always there like the wires bringing power,
Internet, and phone to every house,
connecting them to everywhere.

There is the stop sign that drivers treat
As if they were actors in a Freudian play
Some simply ignore, some slightly hesitate,
And some strictly obey.

There is the house across the street
With its Christmas lights still hanging
The man we've met, wife we've yet to meet,
And a child whom we rarely see out playing.

The house next to them has a new-born
child, Dad works for Apple, mom runs a
summer camp. If you knock on the door the
dog goes wild. By their curb someone left a
bag of dog crap.

A crow thinks he is Cohen's bird on a wire

Two doves whose love, like Morrison said,
can't get much higher. A hummingbird
circling our sage with desire and the car that
just pulled over with a flat tire

So there is my view from my poet's window
Mr. Collins, I just wanted you to know.

# The Beginning

Have you ever stopped to think of the day you were born?
Not the date, but the actual day of the week

For me it was a Sunday which makes me
A child full of grace or so they say

Was my birthday an omen, foretelling one day
I would be a man of the cloth leading others to pray?

What was my mother planning that day?
Was she on her way to a church somewhere?

Was my father planning to fish that day,
An omen that he did not really care?

My older sister was not yet four
So, was I a surprise or had they planned for more?

These are questions that twirl in my head
Answers left open as both my parents are dead

Whatever was happening on that Sunday
I have only one thing to say, thanks mom
and dad for not giving me away.

# On Writing Poetry

Ideas for poems can come from anywhere
The simplest being from the flight of a bird
The rolling tide, or the laziness of a cat

Reading other poets brings poems to mind
Not stealing their lines but reading words
That make me think also of this or that

Poems don't always have to rhyme
No need to match line after line
This one doesn't need to end in hat or mat

But the strangest thing in writing poetry
Is the poem that begins to form in one's mind
Is never the same when pen and paper react.

# Two Ducks

Walking the beach everyday
A routine I hope never to take for granted
I am always amazed by the sights
We find along the shore ever so slanted

One day might be a seal, one day a whale
Sometimes an otter or two, or sometimes
On the horizon a boat with a sail

Sometimes we are surprised by what we find
Like a lost passport, that one time
But what I never thought we would find

Were two ducks walking along the tide
A male and female strolling side by side

Did they not know this water was salt?
Probably the male did not ask for directions
The female telling him this is your fault

That here the two, meant to be by a lake
Found themselves crashing the seagulls clambake.

# The Battle

There is a battle raging outside my window
An aerial assault reminiscent of
A MIG and an F-15

A dove, lighter and more agile
Playing top-gun with a crow
Black as night and twice her size

There must be a nest nearby
Hidden in a tree with two
Small eggs waiting to burst

The dove protecting her territory
The crow simply looking for a meal
Both fulfilling their destiny

When the crow tries to fly
The dove swoops in attacking
From above, the sun at her back

Feathers fly and then they return
To the wires stretched between the poles
For a break in the action, a pause to regroup

While the dove seems to be winning
The crow sits on the wire with a feather
In its mouth, then spits it out and it floats to the

ground, 32 feet/sec/sec

Finally, the crow decides the neighbors
Garbage can is a better choice for sustenance
It swoops down and begins to dig in the trash

The dove ever watchful stays on the wire
One eye on the crow, the other on her nest
Triumphant, at least today.

# What's In A Name

Funny how cities are known by more than a name
Say San Francisco and you think of cable cars
or Rice-A-Roni, the big apple of course is
New York and the windy city we all know
means Chicago

But then Mardi Gras could mean Rio
or New Orleans unless we add
when the saints go marching in
Seattle makes us think of rain, Fairbanks cold
And of course Boston for anything old

Sports are used to define where we might live
Say Steelers or Pirates and we know where you are
Cowboys or Oilers to distinguish your place
In one of the largest, the Lone Star State

Some cities make us think of fun
Like Vegas or Miami, two places with sun
Some we want to visit, we want to see
Like Hollywood or Washington, D.C.

Most are unknown, at least by the majority
Most like not having the notoriety
Sleepy little towns where life is less chaotic
Where not much happens, nothing exotic

Of all the cities I could choose to live in
I have to admit the one I'm in is my pick
The ocean right here that you can swim in
No teams, no celebs, just an old Concrete Ship.

# Our Cat

Why is it that
Having sat for some time
And just about to get up
Our cat decides to jump in my lap

She had been sitting on the floor
Staring into space, or had been
Perched on the table edge, or on
The rail by the stairs for hours

Did she read my mind, hear my thoughts
As I told myself I better get up
And do whatever it is I was about to do?
And then she decides she could make me stay

She can't just leap up and settle down either
She has to approach me as if she did not know me
Before now, and then onto my lap
She has to turn around a few times before settling

Not being cruel, I let her settle for a minute or two
Wishing I did not have to arouse her just yet
But then I must and she protests with a meow,
A cry that says, "What is wrong with you
My name is Isis, goddess of Egypt
And you are here to serve me, sit down!"

# Musical Moments

The first song I remember was *Love Me Tender*
By the king of rock and roll himself
But the one that I played over and over
On my 45 was *Stagger Lee*

Something about the slow beginning
And then quickening the tempo that intrigued me
That and the story that the song was about.

Maybe the opening lines planted the poetry seed
In my brain, "the night was clear and the moon was
yellow"
Helped me see the beauty in the simplest things

When I hear a song from the past
My mind can recall what I was up to
And emotions rise as nostalgia sets in.

But then there are songs that define my life
And for way too long the one that did
Was, "*I Want To Know What Love Is*"

For longer than I care to admit
The words of this song described
My own heartache and pain.

Until that one day, my wife came into my life

And from then until now, above
All, I now know *"The Power of Love"*

# Fooled Ya'

There was a seal on the beach today
We thought for sure was dead
The rangers had cordoned him, or her, off
With orange cones and a sign near his/her head

Marine animal at rest, do not disturb
Is what the sign by his/her head said
My thought was, is this like when your parents
Said your dog had gone north to a farm
When all along you knew he/she was dead?

We passed the lifeless body feeling sad
Was this the seal that had tracked us almost
Every day as we walked along the shore,
Now lying dead, never to greet us anymore?

On our way back we saw people standing near.
Leave the poor creature alone, we wanted to shout
But then we realized the seal was up, nose in the air
Looking at everyone, wondering what the fuss was about

It truly had been just getting rest, lying asleep
Now trying to decide if it should return to the deep
The moral of the story is the joke was on us
Be more positive, don't just think the worst.

# Wednesday

Is Wednesday really a day
Or is it more of a bridge between
What once was and what is to be?

A connection between all
The possibilities and the ones completed
A respite in the journey of life

Wednesday's child is full of woe
Born to be sad, which makes it more
Of a curse than a day

But would you not be sad if caught between
what once was and what is to be?

That would make you nothing
Neither here nor there
And that would be sad and bad

So if I were born on a Wednesday,
Which I was not it turns out,
I would want to be Spanish

Wednesday in Spanish is Miercoles
Which to me sounds like a miracle
Which is what I would rather be.
Than a child of woe born on a Wednesday.

# Today Is Like Yesterday

Wash, rinse, repeat
The cycle of each day
Tumbling out much the same

The day's events washing over us
Only to be rinsed away as night falls
When another day waits to begin again

What this day brings is mostly set
The coffee will be made, the cats fed
The crossword solved, breakfast eaten

The walk along the beach
Down the same stretch of shoreline
Only different if a whale or dolphin appears

The morning shower, the daily shave
My wife stepping into her writing room
To disappear in a world of mystery and murder

The chores of doing the dishes
Emptying the trash, cleaning the cat box
Checking the bank, email, and Twitter

Today is like yesterday
And tomorrow like today
Life on wash, rinse, repeat

But wait, the phone is ringing
Today we get to see our granddaughter
Turning two, and full of surprises

# Prank

In my youth I was known to pull a prank or two
Nothing really mean like pulling legs off of a frog
Or setting a cat's tail on fire

But pranks that were basically harmless
Where no one got hurt and we had a good laugh
My favorite involved salt and pepper shakers

Almost every diner, unless they were really fancy
Had the same type, hexagon in shape and usually
Sitting off to the side, next to sugar packets
and Tabasco

Now I said I wasn't mean so no,
We did not just loosen the lids, sit back
And watch people ruin their meal

What we did do, was sprinkle a little salt
On the table, slide the shaker to make a pile
And then tilt the shaker so it stood on its edge

The trick was to blow away the excess salt
So now the shaker leaned to one side like
The leaning tower of Pisa

We did the same to the pepper and
Then we sat back to watch the show

Some people jarred the table when they sat
So the shakers simply fell over, no fun in that
But sometimes the people were amazed

How could this thing stay askew?
Is this some kind of new design?
We laughed because we knew

That it only took one grain of salt
To make it stay, one grain of salt
To give us a laugh or two

To this day when I am out to eat
If I see shakers that fit the style
I still set them on edge and simply smile.

# "Tuther Way"

It was 1956 and we had left Idaho
Headed to North Carolina in our
Brand new Chevy station wagon

Two tone, gold and bronze, and
We were going to see the U.S.A.
In our Chevrolet 'til my dad got lost

We were in West Virginia and somehow
He got turned around and lost his bearings
So we stopped a lady and asked for directions

To get back to where we needed to be
She said we needed to go "Tuther Way"
So off we went looking for the sign

We came to the main road and
Were ready to resume the trip
When my mother said, "What had she meant?"

My dad laughed for as a southern boy
He knew what she had said, "Tuther Way"
Was simply the other way.

# You Don't Say, D. K. (5/2020)

By the light of the moon, on the darkest evening of the year, Mr. Murder, affectionately known as demon seed was relentless in his pursuit along the dark rivers of the heart of the city,

whose strange highways were icebound and lightning flashed as he left his hideaway at 77 Shadow Street where the servants of twilight, watchers, waited under the winter moon.

The mask he wore showed the face, the face of fear, for he knew what the night knows, that the bad place where dragon tears and night chills were there for the taking of innocence

From the corner of his eye, the eyes of darkness, he saw dark fall, he heard the voice of the night cry out, "Seize the night."

As time moved with velocity, tick tock, knowing he would be the sole survivor of the shadow fires, the cold fire of the odd apocalypse that shattered the vision of the life expectancy of humanity

He had the key to midnight, which opened the door to December, the forbidden door that caused strangers to fear nothing, planting a false memory and leaving them breathless

He approached the funhouse, the house of thunder with the crooked staircase and the silent corner, the whispering room, where whispers and phantoms kept odd hours

Unaware that he was being watched with the intensity of twilight eyes through the night window by Saint Odd, Brother Odd who stood one door away from heaven

The good guy who thought it odd Thomas was so devoted to Ashley Bell, the husband that had told her, "Your heart belongs to me."

He found it deeply odd and that it was the same
As the writing of Mr. Koontz, forever odd.
To be continued...elsewhere.

# Earthquake

the ground is quaking
earth is moving like water
homes once solid fall

# Fallen

Democrats talk and complain
unable to act, restrained
Republicans seem heartless and cruel
power being their only fuel
The president rambles and spews
if called on his lies, claims fake news
Protesters fill the streets chanting
black lives matter as they are marching
Proud boys told to stand down, stand by
whites are supreme is their cry
The media has forgotten true journalism
talking heads babbling ad nauseam
The West Coast is ablaze, acres on fire
the South flooding, rivers getting higher
A pandemic is raging, thousands are dying
masks are worn, people social distancing
To many it is all a hoax, a liberal joke
a flame the far left just want to stoke
America has lost its care for humanity
the world now looks at us with only pity.

# How Could I Not Love You

How could I not love you, mon cher?
with all of my flaws you still care.
Ours is a love that truly will last,
both of us forgetting loves from our past.
No matter what trials may appear
we know each of us will be there
to stand together facing any fear
life may throw at us, so I ask
How could I not love you?

So, with this rondeaux, I say my dear
as we move together thru the next year
to us is left only the one task
stay true to each other with no mask
not causing anything that would shed a tear.
How could I not love you?

# Vision

My vision has been distorted by television
My vision is in need of revision
My vision has been one of division
Hopefully, my vision is a false vision

# The Process

haIl
WenNefer
o my hearT
tHus says the
bull of the wEst
o you who give Bread
herE begin praises
destroy what was done wronGly against me
when It wept
behiNd the embalming
place the Name of its
gatekeepers the praise I sing of Osis
to the great couNcil
the Great council
by my lord God
Open to me
the booth of the great goD

# The New Pen

I asked her, "How is your new pen?"
"Awesome," she said, "better than Le Pen."
Which she had thought was the crème de la crème
of pens, and now she says that is a fallacy
as she went back to her journal quietly

# Not A One

Cowards all, Republicans and Democrats
politicians so afraid to take a stand
power hungry, controlled by the fat cats
cowards all, Republicans and Democrats
find one that's honest and I'll tip my hat
alas, not a one, not a woman or a man
cowards all, Republicans and Democrats
politicians so afraid to take a stand.

# Maintenance

Oil and
filter
change
Rotate tires
check air
pressure
Measure
tire depth
and brake
wear
Change
engine air
filter
Change
cabin air
filter
Inspect
shocks for
wear and tear

Top off
coolant
and brake
fluid
Check
transmission
fluid

Check
battery
output
Clean
battery
terminals

# I Tried

The cats are alert, a spider they seek
while the moth they missed brushes my cheek
the dawn is just now breaking
and as for dinner what am I making?
so off to the beach down to the shore
seeking to see maybe dolphins maybe more
the book has been read
and as the reviewer said
events have more than been discussed
with so much detail and so much fuss
so my life is one of dispersion like light thru a prism
and this is my meager attempt at nude formalism

# Who? I Wonder

Every morning she stands
just at the water's edge
tide gently lapping at her feet
as the sun peeks above the hills

green hoodie, black bike pants,
orange backpack on her shoulders
the hood always shielding her face
always facing out to sea

What goes thru her mind?
What brings her here every day?
Standing for over an hour
moving only slightly along the shore.

Did she lose someone?
Is she tired of life?
Is she simply a mom
needing quiet for a time?

To ask would be to intrude
to even speak rude
so we pass by in silence
letting the mystery linger

# Free, Free At Last

Social media
the bane of modern society
an idea meant to bring us together
source of jealousy, envy, and despair
a black hole sucking time

Facebook where friends connect
or so it was supposed to be
instead jealousy rears as we see
others living seemingly care free

Envy of not having as many friends
of not being as active or able to travel
despair as we see happy families
knowing ours never can be

Twitter where everyone talks
and no one listens
opinions expressed only to be met
with hate or discord

Life's success based on likes
popularity based on clicks
human interaction replaced
by a series of emojis

So for my own sanity

to preserve my humanity
Facebook deleted
Twitter deactivated

Free, free at last.

# The Artist

The beauty within the soul
Of the artist flows
Onto the canvas

Simple strokes creating whole
Images reflecting the
Complexity of life

Life, love, beauty, now
Combined as the artist
Steps back

# Hometown

the field is gone
covered by JC Penney
space we walked on a path
now lost to the past

the landmarks of Friday night
cruises Foster Freeze and Dairy Belle
removed and long forgotten
along with burgers, five for a dollar

somewhere in this suburban sprawl
lies the house of my youth
now surrounded now so buried
in the expanse I can't find it

the quiet little town of twenty-nine-thousand
so dependent on the nearby air base
now holding over one-hundred-five
no longer tied to the government's teat

standing alone thru time and change
one relic survives amongst the new
Dave's Giant Burgers unchanged unmoved
the best god damn burger you will ever eat.

# Happy

Peale told us
to think positively
Esther said
just align with the universe
Tony tells us
we all have a giant within

all of these and more
telling us how to be happy

sound advice, good intentions
many have followed their path

out of chaos
a different idea has come

okay, maybe not different
but one easy to do

we are told to wash our hands
for at least twenty seconds
the time it takes to sing
the happy birthday song twice

How can we not be happy
if several times a day
we look into the mirror and say

Happy birthday to me
happy birthday to me
happy birthday dear ____
happy birthday to me

Happy birthday to me
happy birthday to me
happy birthday dear ____
happy birthday to me

Imagine how happy
the world would be.

# Oh, If They Only Knew

Seated they wait
each with their own thoughts
music designed for focus
cell phones silenced

waiting for inspiration
assurance amid turmoil
eyes locked
the minister about to speak

What if they could see
into the mind of the shepherd?
What thoughts spin as
the word is expounded?

Looking out the minister thinks-
I hate the way Alice plays the organ
I bet Mrs. Bradley corners me after,
another complaint about my grammar.
Too bad Mary doesn't know Dan
is sleeping with Frances.
Maybe I should tell Bill about his breath.
Odds are high three of them will fall asleep.
If I am lucky Betty will bring something
besides fruit Jello to the potluck
This collar is itchy as hell today.

As the service ends and
the last song is sung
everyone files out
"another great sermon
Pastor, well done."

# A Simple Cure

They taught us about
Jack and Jill going up the hill
we knew the bucket was for water
but we never knew what the water was for

They taught us how to be polite
to say yes ma'am and no sir
to not talk with our mouths full
or chew with our mouths open

They even taught us to brush
our teeth after every meal
to see a dentist twice a year
and be sure and wash behind our ears

They taught us to wash our hands
but what I now realize
they never taught us how
no one gave us directions 'til now

Oh, we knew to use soap and water
but did anyone ever say for how long
imagine if all this time, we had all been
washing our hands for twenty seconds all along

Such a simple task, such a simple ask
how many colds or flu would not be spread
if only someone had simply said
wash until you've sung two happy birthdays
in your head

# "Play Ball!"

in a country
where baseball reigns
I can't watch it

America sings
"take me out to the ball game"
and I cringe

sitting, watching
Field of Dreams
I cried

the ball I could never catch
the bat I could never swing
no position could I ever play

the measure of a man
at least, in my father's eyes
a height I could never reach

# Adelaide

how tight
one must be to
write poetically
as Adelaide Crapsey penned the
cinguain.

# Two Lights

two lights
bouncing up the hill

set a few yards apart.
the morning dark

waiting for the sun
to make an appearance.

the first light
said hello as it passed,

the second
said hello too.

two lights
bouncing up the hill

two talking lights
passing us by.

by the sound
both lights female

we watched
as they faded into darkness

we had never
heard lights talk before.

# Nightmare

Snake
fangs dripping venom
mouth agape

slithering in the air
twirling
coming straight at me

I ran
my heart racing
my body trembling

closer and closer
I cried out
I awoke

My eyes opened
but the snake
was still coming

I lept from the bed
ran to my parent's room

the snake kept coming

I cried for help
my father awoke and spoke

the snake coiled
spun up and out
through the ceiling
disappearing

the nightmare
of a six-year-old

# Death

Sadness does not
come to me easily

tears are shed rarely
usually when someone dies

ironically no tears were shed
when my father died
nor for even my mother

my tears have come
as I watched life depart
from the ones I loved

holding them close
starring into their eyes
as their life departed

each time I wept
knowing it was I
who ended their life.

# How's This, Billy Collins?

My eyes have never seen such beauty
the world was surprised when you appeared

eyes have surprised my world when
you appeared the beauty such was never seen

our lives are a reflection of the past
every second century we reappear

every century lives reappear, a reflection
of the past, we are our second

from Egypt to Europe to the U.S.
we have always found each other

to have always Egypt, Europe, the U.S., to found
other we from each

We found Egypt, surprised was the world
to Europe we reappear each a reflection.
you are our beauty
to the U.S. eyes have appeared such
always past lives of the century
have every second seen never from
my other.

# Quest

The first time
I thought it was real
after all, to what did I
have to compare,
to measure against,
was it not Fate?

delusion did not take long
to reveal itself

the journey continued

The second time
desire clouded the mind
commandments shattered
like a rock thru stained glass
building a foundation of sand

a flame without fuel
could not burn

the journey continued

The third time, the charm
beginning as they should
with a merging of minds
a structure solid in friendship
walls of commonality and respect

soulmates reunited
true love finally found

the journey now complete.

# About The Author

Donald Grant is a husband, cook, cat lover, high-handicap golfer, and poet. Usually in that order.
Living on the Central Coast of California, most days include a walk along the beach with his wife.
Raised as a military brat, he has lived in various parts of the United States and spent several years in North Africa. During his life he has been an engineer, a minister, and small business owner.
He loves to comment on life and when something attracts his attention, he will add his thoughts to a poem or two.

www.ingramcontent.com/pod-product-compliance
Lightning Source LLC
Chambersburg PA
CBHW071926020426
42331CB00010B/2749